Good Behaviour

The Supreme Court and
Article III of the
United States Constitution

Good Behaviour

The Supreme Court and Article III of the United States Constitution

by

Samuel A. Francis

SUNSTONE
PRESS

SANTA FE

Sunstone books may be purchased for educational, business, or sales
promotional use. For information please write: Special Markets Department,
Sunstone Press, P.O. Box 2321, Santa Fe, New Mexico 87504-2321.

Library of Congress Cataloging-in-Publication Data:

Francis, Samuel A., 1935–
  Good behaviour: the Supreme Court and Article III of the United States
  Constitution / by Samuel A. Francis.—1st ed.
     p. cm.
  ISBN: 0-86534-337-3
     1. Judges—United States—Discipline. 2. Good behavior (Law)—United
  States. I. Title.

KF8779 .F73 2001
347.73'2634—dc21   2001049045

Published in   SUNSTONE PRESS
                    Post Office Box 2321
                    Santa Fe, NM 87504-2321 / USA
                    (505) 988-4418 / *orders only* (800) 243-5644
                    FAX (505) 988-1025
                    www.sunstonepress.com

Contents

Contents

Introduction

After the *Bush v. Gore* decision in December 2000 I decided to refresh my knowledge of the United States Constitution. Because of the controversy created by the decision I wanted, primarily, to review Article III, the Article that described the rights and responsibilities of the justices of the Supreme Court.

I knew that justices were appointed for life and believed they could only be impeached if found guilty of a high crime or misdemeanor. When I read Article III I could not find any words that said justices were appointed for life. The words that create a lifetime appointment are "during good Behavior." These words mean that as long as a justice maintains "good Behaviour" he is appointed for life.

I have spelled the word "Behaviour" exactly as it is spelled in the Constitution. The capital "B" is also the same as in the Constitution.

I did not remember ever seeing the words "good Behavior" when I previously read the Constitution. When we studied constitutional law in law school we read Article III several times. Most law schools require that each student take one semester of constitutional law. So I thought I was deficient in my memory of Article III.

Several friends of mine are attorneys, good ones. After I reviewed Article III I decided to see how many of my attorney friends remembered "good Behaviour." I asked six of them when they had last read Article III. Ten years or longer was the common answer. When I asked them about the words "good Behaviour," none of them recalled reading those words.

After discussing the meaning of "good Behaviour" I asked them how they felt about the behaviour of three justices regarding the *Bush v. Gore* decision, Justices Sandra Day O'Connor, Antonin Scalia and Clarence Thomas. Four of the attorneys were Republicans and two were Democrats. They all agreed in their opinion that the three justices did not act with "good Behaviour."

I decided to do an informal survey of people other than attorneys regarding the subject of the Supreme Court of the United States. Some questions I asked were: had they ever read Article III; how many justices are there; what are the names of the justices; who appoints the justices; had they ever heard the term "during good Behaviour." I talked to people in the gym that I attend. I talked to bankers, contractors, doctors and people in many walks of life. None of them had read Article III and never heard the term "good Behaviour" as applied to the justices.

After I did the informal survey I realized few people had ever read Article III and had no knowledge that the justices were appointed during "good Behaviour." So I decided to do some research and write a short book containing a brief history of the United States Constitution, a summary of Article III of the Constitution, the makeup of the Supreme Court, a summary of the probable meaning of "good Behaviour" and a brief analysis of the *Bush v. Gore* decision. I did not intend this to be a comprehensive study of the Constitution and the Supreme Court. Fine authors have already done this. My thought is that maybe this can be used as a guide and that the reader will gain some beneficial knowledge. At the end of this book I have included a copy of the United States Constitution. I believe that it might be important to have a copy of the Constitution on the home bookshelf.

—Samuel A. Francis

1

Establishment of the Three Branches of the United States Government

In 1781 the Articles of Confederation were adopted by the thirteen states. The intent was to bind the states into a workable union. Flaws in the Articles became evident and the states agreed some alterations needed to be made. A convention of state representatives was scheduled in May 1787.

The constitutional convention began on May 14, 1787. Twenty-nine delegates from seven of the thirteen states were in attendance. General George Washington was elected President of the convention. The main issues were the establishment of a Congress, the creation of an executive branch of government and a national judiciary.

A great disparity in population between the large and small states was the most divisive issue in the convention. The concern revolved around representation in the two houses of Congress. Debate took place on the selection of members of the Senate and the House. The number of senators from each state and the number of House members from each state consumed a lot of energy of the delegates. Some of the delegates wanted the members of the Senate and the House to be selected on the basis of population. Some wanted each to have only one vote in the Senate. A division between the northern and southern states arose when the question of including slaves in the population count was raised.

On Monday July 16, 1787 the Great Compromise was reached. Legislative powers were vested in the Congress of the United States that was to consist of a Senate and a House of Representatives. Each state, regardless of size, would have two senators, which provided the states with an equal vote. The members of the House of Representatives would be selected based upon the free population of each state plus two-thirds of the slave population of each state. Members of the House would be democratically elected by the people of each state and senators would be elected by the legislature of their respective states. Members of the House were to be elected every two years. The Senate members were to serve for six years. Because the Senate members were not subject to the popular vote, it was thought that they would be the stabilizing forces in the new constitutional government.

Article I of the new Constitution provided the method of election of the United States Congress and enumerated the duties and powers of the new Congress.

The convention began the debate on the issue of executive power on June 1, 1787. Delegates were unable to decide on how many men should occupy the executive position. Some of them wanted one person and others felt that a three men executive would be best. As the debate on how many men should occupy the executive position came to a standstill, the debate shifted to the method of election.

On July 17, 1787 the states voted that the executive position consist of a single person. Debate continued on how to elect that executive and how long the term of the executive would be. Proposals were introduced calling for the method of electing the executive. One wanted the executive to be elected by the national legislature. Another wanted the election to be by the people of each state. Some delegates wanted the executive to be elected for a single seven-year term.

On September 12, the convention finally adopted a plan for the election of a national executive. The executive would be elected for a term of four years and would be chosen by electors who would be chosen by the state legislators. The plan also included a vice-president. Article II became the final proposal for the executive branch of government.

Relatively little time was spent by the delegates debating the structure and power of a national judiciary. The delegates who drafted the final version of the Constitution's national judiciary displayed extraordinary unity. They were united in granting the judiciary expansive powers over state and federal legislation. They vested the Supreme Court with powers that made it the dominant branch of the new national government.

Once the power issues were decided, the method of appointing judges became the next controversy. Some wanted the judges for all federal courts to be appointed by the national legislature. Other delegates supported a selection by the national executive. A third alternative was that the Senate makes the judicial appointments. The final outcome gave the authority to the President to appoint the members of the Supreme Court, provided that two-thirds of the members of the Senate concur.

The original Constitution of the United States was adopted on September 17, 1787. The ratification by the individual states was completed on June 21, 1788. The original Constitution contained seven articles.

Here is Article III:

Section I. The judicial power of the United States, shall be vested in one Supreme Court, and in such inferior courts as the Congress may from time to time ordain and establish. The judges, both of the supreme and inferior courts, shall hold their offices during good Behaviour, and shall, at stated times receive for their services, a compensation, which shall not be diminished during their continuance in office.

Section 2. The judicial power shall extend to all cases, in law and equity, arising under this Constitution, the laws of the United

States, and treaties made, or which shall be made, under their authority:—to all cases affecting ambassadors, other public ministers and consuls;—to all cases of admiralty and maritime jurisdiction;—to controversies to which the United States shall be a party;—to controversies between two or more states;—between a state and citizens of another state;—between citizens of different states;—between citizens of the same state claiming lands under grants of different states, and between a state, or the citizens thereof , and foreign states, citizens or subjects.

In all cases affecting ambassadors, other public ministers and consuls, and those in which a state shall be party, the Supreme Court shall have original jurisdiction. In all other cases before mentioned, the Supreme Court shall have appellate jurisdiction, both as to law and fact, with such exceptions, and under such regulations as the Congress shall make. The trial of all crimes, except in cases of impeachment, shall be by jury; and such trial shall be held in the state where the said crimes shall have been committed; but when not committed within any state, the trial shall be at such place or places as the Congress may by law have directed.

Section 3. Treason against the United States shall consist only in levying war against them, or in adhering to their enemies, giving them aid and comfort. No person shall be convicted of treason unless on the testimony of two witnesses to the same overt act, or confession in open court. The Congress shall have power to declare the punishment of treason, but no attainder of treason shall work corruption of blood, or forfeiture except during the life of the person attainted.

On February 1, 1790 the Supreme Court had six members, a number the Congress had established in the Judiciary Act of 1789. President George Washington appointed these first members.

Through the years the size of the Court increased to seven and then to nine. In 1863, during President Lincoln's administration the Congress increased the number to ten. This move to ten has been described as a "judicial bonus" to President Lincoln. Congress reduced the Court to seven in 1866.

Then in 1869 the number was returned to nine.

In February 2001 the Supreme Court was composed of the following individuals, seven of the justices appointed by republican presidents and two appointed by a democrat president.

William Hobbs Rehnquist, Chief Justice, appointed by President Richard Nixon in 1972. In 2001 he was in his thirtieth year on the bench. He was proud of being called a conservative partisan.

In 1975 President Gerald Ford appointed John Paul Stevens to the Court. He was acknowledged as a judicial moderate.

Sandra Day O'Connor, the first woman to serve on the Court, appointed by President Ronald Reagan in 1981 was considered a judicial conservative.

President Reagan appointed his second justice in 1986, Antonin Scalia. He was considered to be a conservative partisan, with leanings to the right of Chief Justice Rehnquist.

In 1988 President Reagan appointed his third justice, Anthony McLeod Kennedy who was considered to be more of a moderate than Reagan's other appointees.

President George Bush's first appointment in 1990 was David H. Souter. Even though he was appointed by a conservative president, Souter was considered somewhat of a centrist justice.

The second appointment by President Bush in 1991 was Clarence Thomas. He is a black justice and considered being as conservative as any justice on the Court.

President Bill Clinton appointed the second woman to the Court, Ruth Bader Ginsburg, in 1993. She has been described as a cautious liberal.

Another cautious liberal was appointed by President Clinton in 1994, Stephen G. Breyer.

The length of time a justice shall serve is described in Article III "The judges, both of the supreme and inferior courts, shall hold their offices during "good Behaviour." Throughout the history of the United States no one has been sure of what the term "good Behaviour" means.

2

The Meaning of "good Behaviour"

The Constitution provides in Article II, Section 4, that "The President, Vice President and all other civil officers of the United States shall be removed from Office on Impeachment for, and conviction of, Treason, Bribery, or other high Crimes and Misdemeanors." Supreme Court Justices are included in the category of "civil officers."

Congress has the power to begin the procedure for removing a Supreme Court Justice who may be accused of an offense listed in Article II. If charges are brought before the Congress, a majority vote of the congressional members is sufficient to impeach the person charged. Subsequent to the impeachment the charges go before the full Senate. The Senate votes to determine the guilt or innocence of the accused. If the person is found guilty, he or she will be removed from office. If found innocent that person will remain in office.

Soon after the adoption of the Constitution the issue of the meaning of "good Behaviour" was challenged. The main question was whether "good Behaviour" could only be violated by committing offenses listed in Article II. There is some clouded precedent that allows impeachment for behavior other than the Article II provisions.

In March of 1804 the United States House of Representatives voted to impeach Justice Samuel Chase who had been appointed by President George Washington in 1796. At the time of Chase's impeachment the president was Thomas Jefferson. The president was upset with Justice Chase and wanted him removed from the Court. Justice Chase had violated no criminal laws but his judicial behavior was described as not being good. There was uncertainty regarding the standard to apply to the impeachment charges. The behavior of Justice Chase was challenged as violating the "good Behaviour" provision of Article III.

Chase's trial began in January 1805 in the Senate chambers. The House filed eight articles of impeachment. They were all politically motivated. After a one-month trial the Senate voted to acquit Chase of all eight charges.

The Chase case is the last impeachment proceeding against a Supreme Court Justice. The reasons for his impeachment and the acquittal do not settle the meaning of "good Behaviour." Members of the Senate and the House are not sure what type of behavior is cause for impeachment. Must the behavior be in the form of a high crime or misdemeanor? Even though some questionable behavior was displayed in the *Bush v. Gore* case in the year 2000, no person of authority raised the issue of "good Behaviour."

Some constitutional scholars have questioned the type of behavior that would be cause for impeachment. So far no consensus has been reached. It appears that the true meaning of "good Behaviour" is an appointment for life or until a justice resigns.

3

Supreme Court Justices Appointed for Life

In 1789 the first justices were appointed to the Supreme Court. At that time the life expectancy was much shorter than it is today. An estimate of male life expectancy in 1789 was fifty years. Today it is about seventy-seven years. One can only wonder if a lifetime appointment would have been created if the life expectancy in 1789 were the same as it is today.

President Washington made the first ten appointments to the Supreme Court. Here is a list of their names and years of service.

	Years of Service	Number of Years
John Jay	1785-1795	6
John Rutledge	1789-1791	2
William Cushing	1789-1810	21

James Wilson	1789-1798	9
John Blair Jr.	1789-1796	7
James Iredell	1790-1799	9
Thomas Johnson	1791-1793	2
William Paterson	1793-1806	13
Samuel Chase	1796-1811	15
Oliver Ellsworth	1796-1800	4

The average time spent on the Court by the ten justices was 8.8 years.

The following names and years of service of the justices that were on the Court in 2001 will show the contrast between the time served in the early years and the year 2001.

	Years of Service	Number of Years
Williams Hubbs Rehnquist	1972-	29
John Paul Stevens	1975-	26
Sandra Day O'Connor	1981-	20
Antonin Scalia	1986-	15
Anthony McLeod Kennedy	1988-	13
David Souter	1990-	11
Clarence Thomas	1991	10
Ruth Bader Ginsburg	1993-	8
Stephen G. Breyer	1994	7

The average years spent on the Court by these justices is 15.44 years. That is close to double the time spent on the Court by the first justices.

President Franklin D. Roosevelt appointed three justices with the longest combined longevity: Justices Hugo Black, Felix Frankfurter and William Douglas. Between them they served for ninety-three years. They wrote three thousand opinions that had a profound effect on American law and society. William Douglas served the longest of any justice in history, thirty-six years. After being crippled by strokes he resigned in 1975 at age of seventy-seven.

When Article III was adopted the idea was to appoint judges for life so that they would not be part of the voting process. Judges would be immune from the pressures of being a person running for office. They could be independent of the executive and legislative branches. Their court decisions were not to be influenced by politics. History has shown that this idea went astray. Every Supreme Court Justice has been selected because of his or her political partisanship. George Washington's party was the Federalist Party. All of the justices he appointed were from the Federalist Party. President Raegan appointed republicans to the Court and so did President Bush. President Clinton appointed democrats.

In more modern times it sometimes seems that justices are not selected because of their judicial prowess. When the judges appear before the Senate to be approved or not, the questions asked of the appointees sometimes have very little to do with judicial skills. Justice Clarence Thomas is a perfect example. He almost lost approval because of accusations of flirting with a woman. That was the main focus of his hearing before the Senate.

How has the lengthy lifetime appointments to the Court contributed to or overruled the checks and balances theory of the Constitution. The executive branch has checks and balances over the legislature. The President has the power of the veto. The legislature has its checks and balances over the President. The legislature is the only body that can pass legislation. It can also override the President's veto. Are there any checks and balances over the members of the Supreme Court once an individual is appointed to the Court? In the final analysis what government body has the most lasting control over all facets of the United States system, economics, race, religion, politics and more, the Supreme Court.

4

The Constitution's Separation of Powers and Checks and Balances

The only control the President has over the Supreme Court is his right to appoint justices to any vacancy. Beyond that authority the President can do very little to balance the power of the Justices of the Supreme Court.

Some presidents have attempted to balance the Court's power in different ways.

In 1803, as mentioned previously, Thomas Jefferson became the first President to make a concerted effort to have a Supreme Court Justice removed from the Court. Justice Chase remarked to a grand jury that "Jeffersonian mobocracy threatened

to destroy peace and order, freedom and prosperity."
Jefferson, who became hostile to Justice Chase, got
his House leader to work on impeaching the justice.
The House impeached him but the Senate voted to
acquit him. The executive office failed to overpower
the Court.

In 1832 a sitting president ignored a Supreme
Court decision. The case was *Worcester v. Georgia*.
Samuel Worcester, a missionary, was arrested in the
spring of 1831 for violating a Georgia law that made
it a crime for a white man to stay in Indian Territory
without taking an oath to the state of Georgia.
Worcester was in Cherokee territory supporting the
Indians' right to remain in the territory. After his
arrest he refused to take the oath and was sentenced
to four years at hard labor.

His case was appealed to the Supreme Court
and in *Worcester v. Georgia* the Court declared that
the Georgia law on which Worcester was jailed
violated the treaty with the Cherokees, which by the
Constitution was binding on the states. The court
ordered Worcester freed. Georgia ignored the Court
and President Jackson refused to enforce the court
order. Jackson responded harshly to Justice
Marshall's order. "John Marshall has made his
decision. Now let him enforce it."

There was another time in United States history when a President became so frustrated with the Supreme Court that he made an effort to change the structure of the Court.

During his first administration, Franklin D. Roosevelt suffered Supreme Court decisions that interfered with his "new deal" policies. He believed, and so did others from his side, that his policies were needed for the nation's economic improvement. After his election for a second term in 1936 he began an effort to pack the Court. His plan, which was referred to as the "judicial reorganization bill," authorized the President to nominate up to fifty new federal judges, one for each sitting judge who failed to resign or retire within six months of his seventieth birthday. No more than six justices could be added to the Supreme Court. There were currently six justices on the Supreme Court over seventy years old.

In March of 1937 an event occurred that began a series of court decisions that changed Roosevelt's need to reorganize the Court. The case of *West Coast Hotel v. Parrish* came before the Supreme Court and was expected to be decided on the basis of a prior decision by the same Supreme Court members. In the prior case, *Morehead v. Tipaldo,* a New York law creating a minimum wage was challenged by Tipaldo, a Brooklyn laundry owner. After New York's highest court upheld Tipaldo's challenge the state appealed to the Supreme Court and lost on appeal. Roosevelt and his "new deal" supporters supported the minimum wage law. They were disappointed by the Supreme Court's decision.

In the *West Coast Hotel* case, the state of Washington's minimum wage law was challenged. It was an identical law as the one challenged in the *Morehead* case. Washington's highest court upheld the law. An appeal to the Supreme Court was accepted but much to everyone's surprise the Court upheld the decision. This was a true victory for President Roosevelt. Shortly after the *West Coast Hotel* case the Supreme Court handed down decisions that supported Roosevelt's agenda. There was no longer a need for Roosevelt's court-packing plan.

President Franklin Roosevelt was elected to the presidency four times. After his death in 1945 during his fourth term, the Congress feared the office of the President had gained too much power. Congress felt that the way to avoid any future Presidents from being elected for such a long term was to amend the Constitution to limit terms a President could serve. Article V of the Constitution gave Congress the power to begin the proceedings to amend the Constitution. Article V:

"The Congress, whenever two-thirds of both houses shall deem it necessary shall propose amendments to this constitution, or on the applications of the legislatures of two-thirds of the several states, shall call a convention for proposing amendments, which, in either case, shall be valid to all intents and purposes, as part of this constitution, when ratified by the legislatures of three- fourths of the several states, or by conventions in three-fourths thereof, as the one or the other mode of ratification may be proposed by the Congress ...."

Congress' efforts produced Amendment XXII that was adopted in 1951.

Amendment XXII:

"No person shall be elected to the office of the President more than twice, and no person who has held the office of President, or acted as President, for more than two years of a term to which some other person was elected President shall be elected to the office of the President more than once. But this Article shall not apply to any person holding the office of the President when this Article was proposed by the Congress, and shall not prevent any person who may be holding the office of President, or acting as President, during the term within which this Article becomes operative from holding the office of President or acting as President during the remainder of such term."

This Amendment was a clear form of checks and balances on the executive branch of government.

Article I of the Constitution defines the power of the Congress. The Senate and the House of Representatives are granted different types of authority over the Supreme Court.

Article I grants to the House the sole power of impeachment. The Senate has the sole power to try all impeachments. This is one of the checks and balances that Congress can enforce on the Supreme Court.

Congress also has the authority to increase or decrease the number of justices on the Court. Under certain Judiciary Acts passed by Congress, the number of justices have been increased and decreased. It has been many years since the number of justices has been less than nine.

For all its power the Supreme Court remains at the mercy of Congress in one other area. Congress has the authority to define the Court's appellate jurisdiction. Article III, Section 2, "…. In all other cases before mentioned the Supreme Court shall have appellate jurisdiction, both as to law and fact, with such exceptions, and under such regulations as the Congress shall make."

However, Congress has limited it interference even during times of acute constitutional controversy.

In 1869 the issue of Congress' authority to limit the appellate jurisdiction of the Supreme Court was raised in the case of *Ex Parte McCardle*. McCardle, a Mississippi newspaper editor, was arrested on charges of publishing incendiary articles, and held for trial by a military commission established by the Reconstruction Acts. His petition for a writ of habeas corpus was denied by the circuit court. When the case went to the Supreme Court and it heard arguments on the case, Congress feared the Court might declare the Reconstruction Acts unconstitutional. Congress quickly legislated to withdraw the Court's appellate jurisdiction over habeas corpus cases that it had granted to the Court only a year earlier.

Chief Justice Chase delivered the unanimous opinion of the Court. The Supreme Court held that Congress is empowered to define the appellate jurisdiction so as to withdraw from the Court even cases raising constitutional issues.

Very soon after the Constitution was adopted the Supreme Court began its role in the checks and balances arena. In the case of *Marbury v. Madison,* decided in 1803, the Court exercised its power to void legislation it believed was unconstitutional.

Prior to his retirement from the presidency, John Adams appointed William Marbury as a justice of the peace, but due to an oversight, his commission was not delivered to him. The new President, Thomas Jefferson, ordered his secretary of state, James Madison, not to deliver the commission to Marbury. Marbury then sued directly to the Supreme Court for a writ of mandamus requiring Madison to give him his commission. A writ of mandamus is an order issued by the court commanding a party to do a particular act. Section 13 of the Judiciary Act of 1789 gave the Supreme Court the power to issue writs of mandamus. Chief Justice Marshall issued the opinion of the Court:

"The question, whether an act, repugnant to the constitution, can become the law of the land, is a question deeply interesting to the United States; but, happily, not of an intricacy proportioned to its interest. It seems only necessary to recognize certain principles, supposed to have been long and well established, to decide it.

"That the people have an original right to establish, for their future government, such principles, as, in their opinion, shall most conduce to their own happiness is the basis on which the whole American fabric has been erected. The exercise of this original right is a very great exertion; nor can it, nor ought it, to be frequently repeated. The principles, therefore, so established, are deemed fundamental. And as the authority from which they proceed is supreme, and can seldom act, they are designed to be permanent.

"This original and supreme will organizes the government, and assigns to different departments their respective powers. It may either stop here, or establish certain limits not to be transcended by those departments.

"The government of the United States is of the latter description. The powers of the legislature are defined and limited; and that those limits may not be mistaken, or forgotten, the constitution is written. To what purpose are powers limited, and to what purpose is that limitation committed to writing, if these limits may, at any time, be passed by those intended to be restrained? The distinction between a government with limited and unlimited powers is abolished, if those limits do not confine the person on whom they are imposed, and if acts prohibited and acts allowed, are of equal obligation. It is a proposition too plain to be contested, that the constitution controls any legislative act repugnant to it; or, that the legislature may alter the constitution by an ordinary act."

The act of Congress that gave the Court original jurisdiction in this type of writ, Justice Marshall declared unconstitutional. The Constitution gives specific original jurisdiction to the Supreme Court in all cases affecting ambassadors, other public ministers and consuls, and those in which a state is a party. But the Constitution mandates in all other cases that the Supreme Court shall have appellate jurisdiction alone. When Congress attempted in the Judiciary Act of 1798 to give original jurisdiction to the Supreme Court over writs of mandamus, Congress acted contrary to the constitutional provision that, in matters such as mandamus, the Supreme Court may only review the acts of the lower courts. A precedent was established that created the now unquestioned power of the Court to declare acts of Congress unconstitutional and, therefore, void. This established precedent has been followed ever since.

In 1983 the Supreme decided another

important separation of powers case, *Immigration and Naturalization Service v. Chada*. This case presented a challenge to the constitutionality of the provision of the Immigration and Nationality Act, authorizing one House of Congress by resolution, to invalidate the decision of the Executive Branch, pursuant to authority delegated by Congress to the Attorney General of the United States, to allow deportable aliens to remain in the United States. The legislators were dissatisfied with a rule drafted by a federal agency. Both Houses of Congress can act to override the agency by canceling the rule and writing a new law. This is a time consuming procedure. During the Hoover administration Congress began a one-house veto of agency rules.

Chada, an East Indian immigrant, was ordered deported following a one-house veto of an Immigration and Naturalization Service action, which would have allowed him to remain in the United States. The court of appeals ruled the congressional veto unconstitutional and the Supreme agreed:

"The choices we discern as having been made in the Constitutional Convention impose burdens on governmental processes that often seem clumsy, inefficient, even unworkable, but those hard choices were consciously made by men who had lived under a form of government that permitted arbitrary governmental acts to go unchecked. There is no support in the Constitution or decisions of this Court for the proposition that the cumbersomeness and delays often encountered in complying with explicit constitutional standards may be avoided, either by the Congress or by the President. With all the obvious flaws of delay, untidiness, and potential for abuse, we have not yet found a better way to preserve freedom than by making the exercise of power subject to the carefully crafted restraints spelled out in the Constitution."

By the year 1952, presidential power had been steadily expanding. In that year, in the case of *Youngstown Sheet and Tube Company v. Sawyer* the Court attempted to put some restraints on presidential power. The main issue of the case was whether the president had a constitutional right to seize private property during a war emergency. President Truman ordered his secretary of commerce to seize the steel companies in order to avert a threatened strike and continue production for the Korean war. Youngstown Sheet and Tube Company and other steel companies appealed to the Supreme Court.

The Court, by a vote of six to three ruled that since the president had no statutory authority for his action, it must be considered void. "....The President's power, if any, to issue the order must stem from an act of Congress or from the Constitution itself. There is no statute that expressly authorizes the President to take possession of property as he did here. Nor is there any act of Congress to which our attention has been directed from which such a power can fairly be implied...."

"....The Founders of this Nation entrusted the lawmaking power to the Congress alone in both good and bad times. It would do no good to recall the historical events, the fears of power and the hopes for freedom that lay behind their choice. Such a review would but confirm our holding that this seizure order cannot stand."

Another important separation of powers case involving the president was *United States v. Nixon (1974)*. An indictment, charging several offenses, was issued by a federal grand jury in the District of Columbia charging several government officials, including two presidential assistants and a former attorney general. President Nixon was named by the grand jury as a co-conspirator. The district court issued a subpoena ordering the president to produce certain tape recordings and documents relating to his conservation with aids and advisers. Nixon's lawyers attempted to quash the subpoenas on the grounds that production of the requested material would violate the president's executive privilege against disclosure of confidential communication.

The district court refused to quash the subpoenas. In July of 1974 the Supreme Court gave the opinion upholding the district court. The court said ".... In this case we must weigh the importance of the general privilege of confidentiality of Presidential communications in performance of responsibilities against the inroads of such a privilege on the fair administration of criminal justice. The interest in preserving confidentiality is weighty indeed and entitled to great respect. However, we cannot conclude that advisers will be moved to temper the candor of their remarks by the infrequent occasions of disclosure because of the possibility that such conversations will be called for in the context of a criminal prosecution.

"....On the other hand, the allowance of the privilege to withhold evidence that is demonstrably relevant in a criminal trial would cut deeply into the guarantee of due process of law and gravely impair the basic function of the courts. A President's acknowledged need for confidentiality in the communications of his office is general in nature, whereas the constitutional need for production of relevant evidence in a criminal proceeding is specific and central to the fair adjudication of a particular criminal prosecution may be totally frustrated. The President's broad interest in confidentiality of communications will not be vitiated by disclosure of a limited number of conversations preliminarily shown to have some bearing on the pending criminal cases....

"We conclude that when the ground for asserting privilege as to subpoenaed materials sought for use in a criminal trial is based only on the generalized interest in confidentiality, it cannot prevail over thefundamental demands of due process of law in the administration of criminal justice. The generalized assertion of privilege must yield to the demonstrated, specific need for evidence in a pending criminal trial."

These cases illustrate the fact that balance of power is weighted in favor of the judicial branch of the United States. The Court has the sole power to declare statutes unconstitutional. Any exercise of power by the executive and legislative branches of government that is challenged is subject to judicial restraint. The only checks on the Court's power are the justices' own self-restraint. Once the Court makes a decision there is no branch of government that can overturn that decision.

Here are two different opinions about the check on Supreme Court power.

In a dissenting opinion in *U.S. v. Butler (1937)* Justice Stone said the following. "The power of courts to declare a statute unconstitutional is subject to two guiding principles of decision which ought never to be absent from judicial consciousness. One is that courts are concerned only with the power to enact statutes, not with their wisdom. The other is that while unconstitutional exercise of power by the executive and legislative branches of the government is subject to judicial restraint, the only check upon our own excessive power is our own sense of self-restraint. For the removal of unwise laws from the statute books appeal lies not to the courts but to the ballot and to the processes of democratic government."

In the same year of 1937 Justice Sutherland responded to the issue of self-restraint in his dissent in the case of *West Coast Hotel v. Parrish*. "The suggestion that the only check upon the exercise of the judicial power, when properly invoked, to declare a constitutional right superior to an unconstitutional statute is the judge's own faculty of self-restraint, is both ill considered and mischievous. Self-restraint belongs in the domain of will and not of judgment. The check upon the judge is that imposed by his oath of office, by the Constitution and by his own conscientious and informed convictions; and since he has the duty to make up his own mind and adjudge accordingly, it is hard to see how there could be any other restraint. This court acts as a unit. It cannot act in any other way, and the majority (whether a bare majority or a majority of all but one of its members) therefore establishes the controlling rule as the decision of the court, binding, so long as it remains unchanged, equally upon those who disagree and upon those who subscribe to it. Otherwise orderly administration of justice would cease. But it is the right of those in the minority to disagree, and sometimes, in matters of grave importance, their imperative duty to voice their disagreement at such length as the occasion demands—always, of course, in terms which, however forceful, do not offend proprieties or impugn the good faith of those who think otherwise.

"It is urged that the question involved should

now receive fresh consideration, among other reasons, because of 'the economic conditions which have supervened'; but the meaning of the Constitution does not change with the ebb and flow of economic events. We frequently are told in more general words that the Constitution must be construed in the light of the present. If by that it is meant that the Constitution is made up of living words that apply to every new condition, which they include, the statement is quite true. But to say, if that be intended, that the words of the Constitution mean today what they did not mean when written—that is, that they do not apply to a situation now to which they would have applied then—is to rob that instrument of the essential element which continues it in force as the people have made it until they and not their official agents, have made it otherwise....

"...The judicial function is that of interpretation; it does not include the power of amendment under the guise of interpretation. To miss the point of difference between the two is to miss all that the phrase "supreme law of the land' stands for, and to convert what was intended as inescapable and enduring mandates into mere moral inflections."

Do the justices believe that interpretation of

the Constitution changes? One justice believed that the Constitution must adapt to changing times. Attending a symposium at Georgetown University in 1985, Justice William J. Brennan gave his opinion on how the Supreme Court should interpret the Constitution.

"We current Justices read the Constitution in the only way we can: as Twentieth Century Americans. We look to the history of the time of framing and to the intervening history of interpretation. But the ultimate question must be, what do the words of the text mean in our time. For the genius of the Constitution rests not in any static meaning it might have had in a world that is dead and gone, but in the adaptability of its great principles to cope with current problems and current needs. What the constitutional fundamentals meant to the wisdom of other times cannot be their measure to the vision of our time."

How do Americans want the Supreme Court to demonstrate "good Behaviour"? Probably the most powerful President of the twentieth century, Franklin D. Roosevelt, had a critical opinion of the Supreme Courts' behavior. In one of his famous "fireside chats" in 1937 he announced the following opinion.

"The Court in addition to the proper use of its judicial functions has improperly set itself up as a third House of the Congress—a super legislature, as one of the justices has called it—reading into the Constitution words and implications that are not there, and which we never intended to be there.

"We have, therefore, reached the point as a Nation where we must take action to save the Constitution from the Court and the Court from itself. We must find a way to take an appeal from the Supreme Court to the Constitution itself. We want a Supreme Court which will do justice under the Constitution—not over it. In our courts we want a government of laws and not of men.

"I want—as all Americans want—an independent judiciary as proposed by the framers of the Constitution. That means a Supreme Court that will enforce the Constitution as written—that will refuse to amend the Constitution by the arbitrary exercise of judicial power—amendment by judicial say-so. It does not mean a judiciary so independent that it can deny the existence of facts universally recognized."

5

The Case of Bush v. Gore
December 2000

One of the most controversial Supreme Court decisions in our history occurred in December 2000: the case of *Bush v. Gore*. It was a case that a majority of legal scholars agree was of a political nature. Many believed that the Supreme Court should not have intervened.

The presidential contest in the year 2000 between George W. Bush and Albert Gore Jr. was one of the closest elections in modern history. A majority of the national popular vote went to Gore, but the electoral vote was not decided until the Supreme Court ruled on the legal issue challenging the vote count in the state of Florida.

The winner of the popular vote in Florida would receive the state's electoral votes that would be enough for either Bush or Gore to have a majority of electoral votes and thus be elected president. Bush received a small majority of the popular votes after the first vote count. Gore challenged the count and asked for a recount of several counties. Florida's Supreme Court ordered the recount to proceed. Bush appealed the Florida court's decision to the United States Supreme Court. Bush feared that a recount would give a majority of the votes to Gore. After two different proceedings before the United States Supreme Court, the Court ruled that the Florida court was wrong and therefore, no recount was allowed, thereby giving the presidency to Bush.

American voters thought the third branch of government, the Supreme Court, would act as a catalyst against divisions in the country. The majority of voters in the country voted for Gore. As the election became a mess, the country turned to the Court, hoping that it would provide wisdom beyond the two bitterly opposed political camps. It didn't happen. The Court seemed as deep into politics as any other branch of government. Especially when one matter before the Court was the outcome of an election in which a main issue was the appointment of future justices.

There has always been pressure on the Supreme Court to appear to rise above political involvement. But the decision that was made was categorized by many as a political decision. The bitter 5-4 decision was one of the most divisive in our nation's history. The dissenters in their opinion not only criticized the decision as being wrong but also dangerous. Justice Steven Breyer warned his colleagues that they "risk a self inflicted wound that may not just harm the court, but the nation."

In decisions prior to the *Bush* case the conservatives on the Court were hardfast on shifting power from the federal government to the states. In this case the justices contradicted their long held states'rights position to reach the result they wanted. The majority struck down the Florida Supreme Courts interpretation of Florida election law.

Whether the majority decision in the *Bush* case was politically motivated, it appeared to be an extension of equal protection. It would seem that legal challenges could be made to all disparities in voting machines and election day procedures. However, the consensus after the decision was that the conservatives in the majority would not likely be receptive to any of these challenges. Even though Supreme Court decisions usually establish precedent to be followed in new cases, the majority used unusual terminology that created doubt about precedent. They said that their decision was limited to the present circumstances. What they effectively said was that the case only applied if you were a presidential candidate whose opponent had persuaded a state court to order a statewide recount without appropriate standards.

The Supreme Court acknowledged that the Florida election code did not violate the U.S. Constitution or other federal law, and that the Florida Court did not change the rules of the election; yet the Supreme Court found a constitutional question in the "problem of equal protection" in the "present circumstance." The circumstance the Supreme Court addressed was the application of the clear-intent-of-the-voter standard in Florida law, a standard common across the country. The Florida code provided that duly constituted election officials in the various counties must apply this standard. If a given county's application of the standard was reasonable, it should stand muster regardless of what another county does, just as, on a notional basis, diverse practices by canvassing committees were accepted in the validation of votes. The practice in each county must provide "equal protection" in the validation of the clear intent of the voters under the jurisdiction of that county's election officials. When the Supreme Court held that the Florida Court should have "adopted adequate statewide standards for determining what is a legal vote," it required the Florida court to reject the legitimate state election code's county-by-county application of the clear-intent standard.

The equal protection clause of Constitutional Amendment IV was enacted to give equal status to freed black slaves. The conservative justices had long been reluctant to apply the laws protection to minorities. Several civil rights advocates pointed out that in the *Bush v. Gore* case, they were eager to provide its protection to a wealthy white political candidate.

The decision in favor of Bush was 5-4. Voting with the majority were Chief Justice William H. Rehnquist, Justices Sandra Day O'Connor, Antonin Scalia, Anthony M. Kennedy and Clarence Thomas. Voting with the minority were Justices John P. Stevens, David Souter, Ruth Bader Ginsburg and Stephen Breyer. Who were these justices on the right and left? How had they voted in the past and what was their stance in the *Bush v Gore* case? Were their opinions politically motivated or governed by the Constitution?

Chief Justice William H. Rehnquist expressed approval of being called a conservative partisan. Rehnquist, a Nixon appointee, generally was seen as a justice aware of the Courts limited enforcement power. His opinions attempted to give deference to the states whenever possible. In the *Bush* case he strayed from his prior leanings.

Justice Sandra Day O'Connor appointed by President Reagan in 1981 was the first woman appointed to the Court. She was known as a conservative with some displays of independence. She preferred the Court stay out of state matters but voted to intervene in state matters in the *Bush* case.

At the time of the 2000 election O'Connor's husband, a Washington attorney, had some health problems. There was speculation that O'Connor wanted to retire to return to Arizona and spend more time with her husband. Newsweek magazine in its' December 25, 2000 edition reported that she attended an election night party on November 7, 2000, with mostly friends and familiar acquaintances. While watching a television set she heard television anchorman Dan Rather call Florida for Al Gore. "This is terrible," she remarked. She commented that the election was over since Gore had already carried two other swing states.

Shortly after she left her place next to her husband, he remarked that his wife was upset because they wanted to retire to Arizona and a Gore win meant they would have to wait another four years. She did not want a democrat to name her successor. Two witnesses described this extraordinary scene to Newsweek Magazine, (December 25, 2000.)

In spite of her declared bias O'Connor voted with the Court majority against Gore. She could have recused herself in an honorable way but then Bush would not have had the votes to prevail. O'Connor would have to remain on the bench if she did not want a democrat president to replace her. Her behavior in this case fueled criticism that justices seek to influence elections. Could it be that she violated the "good Behaviour" clause of Article III?

Justice Anthony M. Kennedy, appointed by President Reagan in 1988 was considered a reliable conservative. On occasion he became one of the Court's swing votes. He made majorities for both liberals and conservatives. One newsmagazine reported that some high court clerks referred to Kennedy as "Flipper". (Newsweek December 25, 2000)

Appointed by President Reagan in 1986, Justice Antonin Scalia had sometimes been described as one of the Courts most irascible justices. Scalia used his rhetoric to attack and ridicule his colleagues. He referred to them and their decisions with unkind adjectives: "irrational," "smug," "preposterous'" "self righteous'" and "lawyer trained elite."

A probability existed that after the 2000 election Chief Justice Rehnquist would retire. During George W.Bush's campaign, candidate Bush commented that the two justices he admired most were Justice Scalia and Justice Thomas. During the election campaign Scalia was quoted as saying he wanted Bush to win the election so that he could be appointed Chief Justice by a republican president.

On December 9, 2000 the same five justices granted Bush a stay of the Florida Supreme Court's mandate allowing the recount. A stay meant that the recount could not proceed. Scalia issued an unusual concurring opinion. He said, " Though it is not customary for the Court to issue an opinion in connection with its grant of a stay, I believe a brief response is necessary to Justice Stevens' dissent. I will not address the merits of the case, since they will shortly be before us in the petition for certiorari that we have granted. It suffices to say that the issuance of the stay suggests that a majority of the Court, while not deciding the issues presented, believe that the petitioner has a substantial probability of success.

"...Another issue in the case, moreover, is the propriety, indeed the constitutionality, of letting the standard for determination of voters' intent—dimpled chads, hangingchads, etc.—vary from county to county, as the Florida Supreme Court opinion, as interpreted by the Circuit Court, permits. If petitioner is correct that counting in this fashion is unlawful, permitting the count to proceed on that erroneous basis will prevent an accurate recount from being conducted on a proper basis later, since it is generally agreed that each manual recount produces a degradation of the ballots, which renders a subsequent recount inaccurate."

Justice Scalia all but declared Bush the winner without hearing oral arguments or without reading the yet to be filed legal briefs. In one paragraph of his opinion he stated, "I will not address the merits of the case." In the paragraph quoted above he did address the merits of the case. The whole issue of the appeal was whether to allow a recount. He determined that a subsequent recount would be inaccurate. The idea of declaring a party the winner without reading the briefs or hearing oral arguments is repugnant to the Constitution.

A disturbing fact surfaced after the decision in *Bush v. Gore*, which gave the presidency to Bush. Time

Magazine, (December 25, 2000), reported that Scalia had two sons that were employed by the law firm that was working on Bush's post election phase. This fact was categorized by many as a conflict of the purest form. Any lower court judge who might have a similar conflict would have asked to be recused. Many said that Scalia should have done just that. Scalia's behavior would suggest another issue of violation of the standard of "good Behaviour."

Another Justice who Bush expressed open admiration for was Justice Clarence Thomas. Bush's father appointed him in 1991. Thomas' supporters referred to him as the leading conservative in America.

After the *Bush v. Gore* decision, Time Magazine in it's December 25, 2000 edition, reported that Thomas' wife worked for the conservative Heritage Foundation where she had been "vetting" resumes for positions in the Bush administration. Mrs. Thomas denied her work was for Bush. Once again another conflict appeared to exist, one that seemed to violate the "good Behaviour" provision.

The oldest member on the Court, at eighty years, was John P. Stevens who was appointed in 1975 by republican President Gerald Ford. Stevens was known as the most liberal member of the Court even though he was appointed by a republican. Stevens wrote a dissenting opinion in the *Bush v. Gore* case. The last paragraph of the dissent was the most critical of the majority. "What must underlie petitioners' entire federal assault on the Florida election procedures is an unstated lack of confidence in the impartiality and capacity of the state judges who would make the critical decisions if the vote count were to proceed. Otherwise, their position is wholly without merit. The endorsement of that position by the majority of the Court can only lend credence to the most cynical appraisal of the work of judges throughout the land. It is the confidence in the men and women who administer the judicial system that is the true backbone of the rule of law. Time will one day heal the wound to that confidence that will be inflicted by today's decision. One thing, however, is certain. Although we may never know with complete certainty the identity of the winner of this year's Presidential election, the identity of the loser is perfectly clear. It is the Nation's confidence in the judge as an impartial guardian of the rule of law."

President Bush appointed Justice David Souter in 1990 who hoped to establish a conservative majority on the Court. The conservative's expectations were not reached because Justice Souter has voted with the liberals on most issues. He was not very vocal in the *Bush v. Gore* case.

President Clinton appointed the second woman to the Supreme Court in 1993. She was Ruth Bader Ginsburg who regularly voted with the liberals. In the Bush v. Gore case she issued a dissent defending state sovereignty. "The Court's conclusion that a constitutionally adequate recount is impractical is a prophecy the Court will not allow to be tested. Such an untested prophecy should not decide the presidency."

Another justice appointed by Clinton in 1994 was Justice Stephen Breyer. He was a cautious jurist who generally voted with the liberals. Here is a quote from his dissent in *Bush v. Gore:* "At the same time, as I have said, the Court is not acting to vindicate a fundamental constitutional principle, such as the need to protect a basic human liberty. No other strong reason to act is present. Congressional statutes tend to obviate the need. And, above all, in this highly politicized matter, the appearance of a split decision runs the risk of undermining the public's confidence in the Court itself. That confidence is a public treasure. It has been built slowly over many years, some of which were marked by a Civil War and the tragedy of segregation. It is a vitally necessary ingredient of any successful effort to protect basic liberty and, indeed the rule of law itself. We run no risk of returning to the days when a President (responding to this Court's efforts to protect the Cherokee Indians) might have said, 'John Marshall has made his decision; now let him enforce it.'....But we do risk a self-inflicted wound—a wound that may harm not just the Court, but the Nation.

"I fear that in order to bring this agonizingly long election process to a definitive conclusion, we have not adequately attended to that necessary 'check upon our exercise of power,' 'our own sense of self-restraint.'"

The Courts' decision was every bit as controversial as the election it resolved. Some of its members attacked the ruling as antidemocratic and politically motivated. Could the Court recover?

6

The Most Powerful Branch of the United States Government

A sizeable number of critics, from lawyers to law professors, attacked the *Bush v. Gore* decision as politically motivated. Some experts and non-experts discovered after the decision the conflicts of some members of the majority. Many expressed opinions that Justices O'Connor, Scalia and Thomas should have recused themselves. They argued that the Supreme Court would have reversed any decision by a lower court judge who had similar conflicts. But no government body can reverse a Supreme Court ruling no matter how serious the conflict.

Other experts argued that there were no clear-cut violations by the justices. They argued the Supreme Court justices could not abstain from the world.

The Court has made mistakes in other decisions in our nations' history. Citizens' support for the Court is damaged when the Court makes a partisan decision. The members of the Court know that they must rise above political divisions.

On January 22, 2001 the newspaper *U.S.A. Today* reported that after the decision the Court received thousands of letters from angry Americans. Some of the words to the justices were sarcastic, others menacing. One letter included an illustration of a skull and crossbones. At times certain justices have been sent letters criticizing a decision. However, it is rare that the entire Court is inundated with letters criticizing the justices. Most of the letters criticized the majority, all republican appointees, for playing politics.

There is an organization called the Supreme Court Bar that consists of attorneys who are eligible to argue before the Supreme Court. Several of the members resigned as protest to the Court's decision. Court officials could not recall lawyers protesting a decision in such a manner.

An article appeared in the conservative

publication, The *Weekly Standard*. "It would be silly to deny that partisan considerations influenced.... the justices ruling." One daily newspaper reported that court insiders indicated the reactions that shook the justices came from Americans who questioned the justices' personal motives. The personal motive issue focused on Justices O'Connor, Scalia and Thomas.

A dialogue began across the nation how to avoid such abuse of judicial power. Many recognized that lifelong appointments were a major factor in the justices' lack of accountability to the country. Although the behavior of Justices O'Connor, Scalia and Thomas was highly criticized there was no call for their resignation or impeachment.

An amendment to the Constitution was the most talked about solution to curtail judicial power. It was an amendment that would limit the number of years a justice could serve on the Court. A justice's partisanship would not be as damaging if his or her time on the Court was limited. The country amended the Constitution to limit the terms of the presidency because it felt that one President became too powerful. Why not apply the same reasoning to the power of the justices?

Most concerned citizens realized that amending the Constitution was a long shot. They sought ways to protect the country from partisan justices. There were not any ways to avoid partisanship on the Supreme Court. Liberals and conservatives realized that the justices are selected on the basis of their political leanings. A large number of Americans voted for the man who would appoint a justice that would represent their political stand. It is a sad story in American history, but many Americans have voted this way in the past and will do so in the future.

Whether or not a change is made to the Supreme Court it will always remain the most powerful branch of the United States Government.

The Constitution of the United States of America

Preamble

We the people of the United States, in order to form a more perfect union, establish justice, insure domestic tranquility, provide for the common defense, promote the general welfare, and secure the blessings of liberty to ourselves and our posterity, do ordain and establish this Constitution for the United States of America.

Article I

Section 1. All legislative powers herein granted shall be vested in a Congress of the United States, which shall consist of a Senate and House of Representatives.

Section 2. The House of Representatives shall be composed of members chosen every second year by the people of the several states, and the electors in each state shall have the qualifications requisite for electors of the most numerous branch of the state legislature.

No person shall be a Representative who shall not have attained to the age of twenty five years, and been seven years a citizen of the United States, and who shall not, when elected, be an inhabitant of that state in which he shall be chosen.

Representatives and direct taxes shall be apportioned among the several states which may be included within this union, according to their respective numbers, which shall be determined by adding to the whole number of free persons, including those bound to service for a term of years, and excluding Indians not taxed, three fifths of all other Persons.

The actual Enumeration shall be made within three years after the first meeting of the Congress of the United States, and within every subsequent term of ten years, in such manner as they shall by law direct. The number of Representatives shall not exceed one for every thirty thousand, but each state shall have at least one Representative; and until such enumeration shall be made, the state of New Hampshire shall be entitled to choose three, Massachusetts eight, Rhode Island and Providence Plantations one, Connecticut five, New York six, New

Jersey four, Pennsylvania eight, Delaware one, Maryland six, Virginia ten, North Carolina five, South Carolina five, and Georgia three.

When vacancies happen in the Representation from any state, the executive authority thereof shall issue writs of election to fill such vacancies.

The House of Representatives shall choose their speaker and other officers; and shall have the sole power of impeachment.

Section 3. The Senate of the United States shall be composed of two Senators from each state, chosen by the legislature thereof, for six years; and each Senator shall have one vote.

Immediately after they shall be assembled in consequence of the first election, they shall be divided as equally as may be into three classes. The seats of the Senators of the first class shall be vacated at the expiration of the second year, of the second class at the expiration of the fourth year, and the third class at the expiration of the sixth year, so that one third may be chosen every second year; and if vacancies happen by resignation, or otherwise, during the recess of the legislature of any state, the executive thereof may make temporary appointments until the next meeting of the legislature, which shall then fill such vacancies.

No person shall be a Senator who shall not have attained to the age of thirty years, and been nine years a citizen of the United States and who shall not, when elected, be an inhabitant of that state for which he shall be chosen.

The Vice President of the United States shall be President of the Senate, but shall have no vote, unless they be equally divided.

The Senate shall choose their other officers, and also a President pro tempore, in the absence of the Vice President, or when he shall exercise the office of President of the United States.

The Senate shall have the sole power to try all impeachments. When sitting for that purpose, they shall be on oath or affirmation. When the President of the United States is tried, the Chief Justice shall preside: And no person shall be convicted without the concurrence of two thirds of the members present.

Judgment in cases of impeachment shall not extend further than to removal from office, and disqualification to hold and enjoy any office of honor, trust or profit under the United States: but the party convicted shall nevertheless be liable and subject to indictment, trial, judgment and punishment, according to law.

Section 4. The times, places and manner of

holding elections for Senators and Representatives, shall be prescribed in each state by the legislature thereof; but the Congress may at any time by law make or alter such regulations, except as to the places of choosing Senators.

The Congress shall assemble at least once in every year, and such meeting shall be on the first Monday in December, unless they shall by law appoint a different day.

Section 5. Each House shall be the judge of the elections, returns and qualifications of its own members, and a majority of each shall constitute a quorum to do business; but a smaller number may adjourn from day to day, and may be authorized to compel the attendance of absent members, in such manner, and under such penalties as each House may provide.

Each House may determine the rules of its proceedings, punish its members for disorderly behavior, and, with the concurrence of two thirds, expel a member.

Each House shall keep a journal of its proceedings, and from time to time publish the same, excepting such parts as may in their judgment require secrecy; and the yeas and nays of the members of either House on any question shall, at the desire of one fifth of those present, be entered on the journal.

Neither House, during the session of Congress, shall, without the consent of the other, adjourn for more than three days, nor to any other place than that in which the two Houses shall be sitting.

Section 6. The Senators and Representatives shall receive a compensation for their services, to be ascertained by law, and paid out of the treasury of the United States. They shall in all cases, except treason, felony and breach of the peace, be privileged from arrest during their attendance at the session of their respective Houses, and in going to and returning from the same; and for any speech or debate in either House, they shall not be questioned in any other place.

No Senator or Representative shall, during the time for which he was elected, be appointed to any civil office under the authority of the United States, which shall have been created, or the emoluments whereof shall have been increased during such time: and no person holding any office under the United States, shall be a member of either House during his continuance in office.

Section 7. All bills for raising revenue shall originate in the House of Representatives; but the Senate may propose or concur with amendments as on other Bills.

Every bill which shall have passed the House of Representatives and the Senate, shall, before it become a law, be presented to the President of the United States; if he approve he shall sign it, but if not he shall return it, with his objections to that House in which it shall have originated, who shall enter the objections at large on their journal, and proceed to reconsider it. If after such reconsideration two thirds of that House shall agree to pass the bill, it shall be sent, together with the objections, to the other House, by which it shall likewise be reconsidered, and if approved by two thirds of that House, it shall become a law. But in all such cases the votes of both Houses shall be determined by yeas and nays, and the names of the persons voting for and against the bill shall be entered on the journal of each House respectively. If any bill shall not be returned by the President within ten days (Sundays excepted) after it shall have been presented to him, the same shall be a law, in like manner as if he had signed it, unless the Congress by their adjournment prevent its return, in which case it shall not be a law.

Every order, resolution, or vote to which the concurrence of the Senate and House of Representatives may be necessary (except on a question of adjournment) shall be presented to the President of the United States; and before the same shall take effect, shall be approved by him, or being disapproved by him, shall be repassed by two thirds of the Senate and House of Representatives, according to the rules and limitations prescribed in the case of a bill.

Section 8. The Congress shall have power to lay and collect taxes, duties, imposts and excises, to pay the debts and provide for the common defense and general welfare of the United States; but all duties, imposts and excises shall be uniform throughout the United States;

To borrow money on the credit of the United States;

To regulate commerce with foreign nations, and among the several states, and with the Indian tribes;

To establish a uniform rule of naturalization, and uniform laws on the subject of bankruptcies throughout the United States;

To coin money, regulate the value thereof, and of foreign coin, and fix the standard of weights and measures;

To provide for the punishment of counterfeiting the securities and current coin of the United States;

To establish post offices and post roads;

To promote the progress of science and useful arts, by securing for limited times to authors and inventors the exclusive right to their respective writings and discoveries;

To constitute tribunals inferior to the Supreme Court;

To define and punish piracies and felonies committed on the high seas, and offenses against the law of nations;

To declare war, grant letters of marque and reprisal, and make rules concerning captures on land and water;

To raise and support armies, but no appropriation of money to that use shall be for a longer term than two years;

To provide and maintain a navy;

To make rules for the government and regulation of the land and naval forces;

To provide for calling forth the militia to execute the laws of the union, suppress insurrections and repel invasions;

To provide for organizing, arming, and disciplining, the militia, and for governing such part of them as may be employed in the service of the United States, reserving to the states respectively, the appointment of the officers, and the authority of training the militia according to the discipline prescribed by Congress;

To exercise exclusive legislation in all cases

whatsoever, over such District (not exceeding ten miles square) as may, by cession of particular states, and the acceptance of Congress, become the seat of the government of the United States, and to exercise like authority over all places purchased by the consent of the legislature of the state in which the same shall be, for the erection of forts, magazines, arsenals, dockyards, and other needful buildings;—And To make all laws which shall be necessary and proper for carrying into execution the foregoing powers, and all other powers vested by this Constitution in the government of the United States, or in any department or officer thereof.

Section 9. The migration or importation of such persons as any of the states now existing shall think proper to admit, shall not be prohibited by the Congress prior to the year one thousand eight hundred and eight, but a tax or duty may be imposed on such importation, not exceeding ten dollars for each person.

The privilege of the writ of habeas corpus shall not be suspended, unless when in cases of rebellion or invasion the public safety may require it.

No bill of attainder or ex post facto Law shall be passed.

No tax or duty shall be laid on articles exported from any state.

No preference shall be given by any regulation of commerce or revenue to the ports of one state over those of another: nor shall vessels bound to, or from, one state, be obliged to enter, clear or pay duties in another.

No money shall be drawn from the treasury, but in consequence of appropriations made by law; and a regular statement and account of receipts and expenditures of all public money shall be published from time to time.

No title of nobility shall be granted by the United States: and no person holding any office of profit or trust under them, shall, without the consent of the Congress, accept of any present, emolument, office, or title, of any kind whatever, from any king, prince, or foreign state.

Section 10. No state shall enter into any treaty, alliance, or confederation; grant letters of marque and reprisal; coin money; emit bills of credit; make anything but gold and silver coin a tender in payment of debts; pass any bill of attainder, ex post facto law, or law impairing the obligation of contracts, or grant any title of nobility.

No state shall, without the consent of the Congress, lay any imposts or duties on imports or exports, except what may be absolutely necessary for executing it's inspection laws: and the net produce of all duties and imposts, laid by any state on imports or exports, shall be for the use of the treasury of the United States; and all such laws shall be subject to the revision and control of the Congress.

No state shall, without the consent of Congress, lay any duty of tonnage, keep troops, or ships of war in time of peace, enter into any agreement or compact with another state, or with a foreign power, or engage in war, unless actually invaded, or in such imminent danger as will not admit of delay.

Article II

Section 1. The executive power shall be vested in a President of the United States of America. He shall hold his office during the term of four years, and, together with the Vice President, chosen for the same term, be elected, as follows:

Each state shall appoint, in such manner as the Legislature thereof may direct, a number of electors, equal to the whole number of Senators and Representatives to which the State may be entitled in the Congress: but no Senator or Representative, or person holding an office of trust or profit under the United States, shall be appointed an elector.

The electors shall meet in their respective states, and vote by ballot for two persons, of whom one at least shall not be an inhabitant of the same state with themselves. And they shall make a list of all the persons voted for, and of the number of votes for each; which list they shall sign and certify, and transmit sealed to the seat of the government of the United States, directed to the President of the Senate. The President of the Senate shall, in the presence of the Senate and House of Representatives, open all the certificates, and the votes shall then be counted. The person having the greatest number of votes shall be the President, if such number be a majority of the whole number of electors appointed; and if there be more than one who have such majority, and have an equal number of votes, then the House of Representatives shall immediately choose by ballot one of them for President; and if no person have a majority, then from the five highest on the list the said House shall in like manner choose the President. But in choosing the President, the votes shall be taken by States, the representation from each state having one vote; A quorum for this purpose shall consist of a member or members from two thirds of the states, and a majority of all the states shall be necessary to a choice. In every case, after the choice of the

President, the person having the greatest number of votes of the electors shall be the Vice President. But if there should remain two or more who have equal votes, the Senate shall choose from them by ballot the Vice President.

The Congress may determine the time of choosing the electors, and the day on which they shall give their votes; which day shall be the same throughout the United States.

No person except a natural born citizen, or a citizen of the United States, at the time of the adoption of this Constitution, shall be eligible to the office of President; neither shall any person be eligible to that office who shall not have attained to the age of thirty five years, and been fourteen Years a resident within the United States.

In case of the removal of the President from office, or of his death, resignation, or inability to discharge the powers and duties of the said office, the same shall devolve on the Vice President, and the Congress may by law provide for the case of removal, death, resignation or inability, both of the President and Vice President, declaring what officer shall then act as President, and such officer shall act accordingly, until the disability be removed, or a President shall be elected.

The President shall, at stated times, receive for his services, a compensation, which shall neither be increased nor diminished during the period for which he shall have been elected, and he shall not receive within that period any other emolument from the United States, or any of them.

Before he enter on the execution of his office, he shall take the following oath or affirmation:—"I do solemnly swear (or affirm) that I will faithfully execute the office of President of the United States, and will to the best of my ability, preserve, protect and defend the Constitution of the United States."

Section 2. The President shall be commander in chief of the Army and Navy of the United States, and of the militia of the several states, when called into the actual service of the United States; he may require the opinion, in writing, of the principal officer in each of the executive departments, upon any subject relating to the duties of their respective offices, and he shall have power to grant reprieves and pardons for offenses against the United States, except in cases of impeachment.

He shall have power, by and with the advice and consent of the Senate, to make treaties, provided two thirds of the Senators present concur; and he shall nominate, and by and with the advice and consent of the Senate, shall appoint ambassadors, other public ministers and consuls, judges of the Supreme Court, and all other officers of the United States, whose appointments are not herein otherwise provided for, and which shall be established by law: but the Congress may by law vest the appointment of such inferior officers, as they think proper, in the President alone, in the courts of law, or in the heads of departments.

The President shall have power to fill up all vacancies that may happen during the recess of the Senate, by granting commissions which shall expire at the end of their next session.

Section 3. He shall from time to time give to the Congress information of the state of the union, and recommend to their consideration such measures as he shall judge necessary and expedient; he may, on extraordinary occasions, convene both Houses, or either of them, and in case of disagreement between them, with respect to the time of adjournment, he may adjourn them to such time as he shall think proper; he shall receive ambassadors and other public ministers; he shall take care that the laws be faithfully executed, and shall commission all the officers of the United States.

Section 4. The President, Vice President and

all civil officers of the United States, shall be removed from office on impeachment for, and conviction of, treason, bribery, or other high crimes and misdemeanors.

Article III

Section 1. The judicial power of the United States, shall be vested in one Supreme Court, and in such inferior courts as the Congress may from time to time ordain and establish. The judges, both of the supreme and inferior courts, shall hold their offices during good Behaviour, and shall, at stated times, receive for their services, a compensation, which shall not be diminished during their continuance in office.

Section 2. The judicial power shall extend to all cases, in law and equity, arising under this Constitution, the laws of the United States, and treaties made, or which shall be made, under their authority;—to all cases affecting ambassadors, other public ministers and consuls;—to all cases of admiralty and maritime jurisdiction;—to controversies to which the United States shall be a party;—to controversies between two or more states;—between a state and citizens of another state;—between citizens of different states;—between citizens of the same state claiming lands under grants of different states, and between a state, or the citizens thereof, and foreign states, citizens or subjects.

In all cases affecting ambassadors, other public ministers and consuls, and those in which a state shall be party, the Supreme Court shall have original jurisdiction. In all the other cases before mentioned, the Supreme Court shall have appellate jurisdiction, both as to law and fact, with such exceptions, and under such regulations as the Congress shall make.

The trial of all crimes, except in cases of impeachment, shall be by jury; and such trial shall be held in the state where the said crimes shall have been committed; but when not committed within any state, the trial shall be at such place or places as the Congress may by law have directed.

Section 3. Treason against the United States, shall consist only in levying war against them, or in adhering to their enemies, giving them aid and comfort. No person shall be convicted of treason unless on the testimony of two witnesses to the same overt act, or on confession in open court.

The Congress shall have power to declare the punishment of treason, but no attainder of treason shall work corruption of blood, or forfeiture except during the life of the person attainted.

Article IV

Section 1. Full faith and credit shall be given in each state to the public acts, records, and judicial proceedings of every other state. And the Congress may by general laws prescribe the manner in which such acts, records, and proceedings shall be proved, and the effect thereof.

Section 2. The citizens of each state shall be entitled to all privileges and immunities of citizens in the several states.

A person charged in any state with treason, felony, or other crime, who shall flee from justice, and be found in another state, shall on demand of the executive authority of the state from which he fled, be delivered up, to be removed to the state having jurisdiction of the crime.

No person held to service or labor in one state, under the laws thereof, escaping into another, shall, in consequence of any law or regulation therein, be discharged from such service or labor, but shall be delivered up on claim of the party to whom such service or labor may be due.

Section 3. New states may be admitted by the Congress into this union; but no new states shall be formed or erected within the jurisdiction of any other state; nor any state be formed by the junction of two or more states, or parts of states, without the consent of the legislatures of the states concerned as well as of the Congress.

The Congress shall have power to dispose of and make all needful rules and regulations respecting the territory or other property belonging to the United States; and nothing in this Constitution shall be so construed as to prejudice any claims of the United States, or of any particular state.

Section 4. The United States shall guarantee to every state in this union a republican form of government, and shall protect each of them against invasion; and on application of the legislature, or of the executive (when the legislature cannot be convened) against domestic violence.

Article V

The Congress, whenever two thirds of both houses shall deem it necessary, shall propose amendments to this Constitution, or, on the application of the legislatures of two thirds of the several states, shall call a convention for proposing amendments, which, in either case, shall be valid to all intents and purposes, as part of this Constitution, when ratified by the legislatures of three fourths of the several states, or by conventions in three fourths thereof, as the one or the other mode of ratification may be proposed by the Congress; provided that no amendment which may be made prior to the year one thousand eight hundred and eight shall in any manner affect the first and fourth clauses in the ninth section of the first article; and that no state, without its consent, shall be deprived of its equal suffrage in the Senate.

Article VI

All debts contracted and engagements entered into, before the adoption of this Constitution, shall be as valid against the United States under this Constitution, as under the Confederation.

This Constitution, and the laws of the United States which shall be made in pursuance thereof; and all treaties made, or which shall be made, under the authority of the United States, shall be the supreme law of the land; and the judges in every state shall be bound thereby, anything in the Constitution or laws of any State to the contrary notwithstanding.

The Senators and Representatives before mentioned, and the members of the several state legislatures, and all executive and judicial officers, both of the United States and of the several states, shall be bound by oath or affirmation, to support this

Constitution; but no religious test shall ever be required as a qualification to any office or public trust under the United States.

Article VII

The ratification of the conventions of nine states, shall be sufficient for the establishment of this Constitution between the states so ratifying the same.

Done in convention by the unanimous consent of the states present the seventeenth day of September in the year of our Lord one thousand seven hundred and eighty seven and of the independence of the United States of America the twelfth.

In witness whereof We have hereunto subscribed our Names,   George Washington,
President and deputy from Virginia.

New Hampshire: John Langdon,
Nicholas Gilman.

Massachusetts: Nathaniel Gorham,
Rufus King.

Connecticut: William Samuel Johnson,
Roger Sherman.

New York:	Alexander Hamilton.
New Jersey:	William Livingston,
	David Brearley,
	William Paterson,
	Jonathan Dayton.
Pennsylvania:	Benjamin Franklin,
	Thomas Mifflin,
	Robert Morris,
	George Clymer,
	Thomas FitzSimons,
	Jared Ingersoll,
	James Wilson,
	Gouverneur Morris.
Delaware:	George Read,
	Gunning Bedford Jr.,
	John Dickinson,
	Richard Bassett,
	Jacob Broom.
Maryland:	James McHenry,
	Daniel of St. Thomas Jenifer,
	Daniel Carroll.
Virginia:	John Blair,
	James Madison Jr.

North Carolina: William Blount,
　　　　　　　　Richard Dobbs Spaight,
　　　　　　　　Hugh Williamson.

South Carolina: John Rutledge,
　　　　　　　　Charles Cotesworth Pinckney,
　　　　　　　　Charles Pinckney,
　　　　　　　　Pierce Butler.

Georgia: 　　　　William Few,
　　　　　　　　Abraham Baldwin.

The Ten Original Amendments: The Bill of Rights.

Passed by Congress September 25, 1789.
Ratified December 15, 1791.

Amendment I

Congress shall make no law respecting an establishment of religion, or prohibiting the free exercise thereof; or abridging the freedom of speech, or of the press; or the right of the people peaceably to assemble, and to petition the government for a redress of grievances.

Amendment II

A well regulated militia, being necessary to the security of a free state, the right of the people to keep and bear arms, shall not be infringed.

Amendment III

No soldier shall, in time of peace be quartered in any house, without the consent of the owner, nor in time of war, but in a manner to be prescribed by law.

Amendment IV

The right of the people to be secure in their persons, houses, papers, and effects, against unreasonable searches and seizures, shall not be violated, and no warrants shall issue, but upon probable cause, supported by oath or affirmation, and particularly describing the place to be searched, and the persons or things to be seized.

Amendment V

No person shall be held to answer for a capital, or otherwise infamous crime, unless on a presentment or indictment of a grand jury, except in cases arising in the land or naval forces, or in the militia, when in actual service in time of war or public danger; nor shall any person be subject for the same offense to be twice put in jeopardy of life or limb; nor shall be compelled in any criminal case to be a witness against himself, nor be deprived of life, liberty, or property, without due process of law; nor shall private property be taken for public use, without just compensation.

Amendment VI

In all criminal prosecutions, the accused shall enjoy the right to a speedy and public trial, by an impartial jury of the state and district wherein the crime shall have been committed, which district shall have been previously ascertained by law, and to be informed of the nature and cause of the accusation; to be confronted with the witnesses against him; to have compulsory process for obtaining witnesses in his favor, and to have the assistance of counsel for his defense.

Amendment VII

In suits at common law, where the value in controversy shall exceed twenty dollars, the right of trial by jury shall be preserved, and no fact tried by a jury, shall be otherwise reexamined in any court of the United States, than according to the rules of the common law.

Amendment VIII

Excessive bail shall not be required, nor excessive fines imposed, nor cruel and unusual punishments inflicted.

Amendment IX

The enumeration in the Constitution, of certain rights, shall not be construed to deny or disparage others retained by the people.

Amendment X

The powers not delegated to the United States by the Constitution, nor prohibited by it to the states, are reserved to the states respectively, or to the people.

Amendment XI

Passed by Congress March 4, 1794. Ratified February 7, 1795.

The judicial power of the United States shall not be construed to extend to any suit in law or equity, commenced or prosecuted against one of the United States by citizens of another state, or by citizens or subjects of any foreign state.

Amendment XII

Passed by Congress December 9, 1803. Ratified July 27, 1804

The electors shall meet in their respective states and vote by ballot for President and Vice-President, one of whom, at least, shall not be an inhabitant of the same state with themselves; they shall name in their ballots the person voted for as President, and in distinct ballots the person voted for as Vice-President, and they shall make distinct lists of all persons voted for as President, and of all persons voted for as Vice-President, and of the number of votes for each, which lists they shall sign and certify, and transmit sealed to the seat of the government of the United States, directed to the President of the Senate;—The President of the Senate shall, in the presence of the Senate and House of Representatives, open all the certificates and the votes shall then be counted;— the person having the greatest number of votes for President, shall be the President, if such number be a majority of the whole number of electors appointed; and if no person have such majority, then from the persons having the highest numbers not exceeding three on the list of those voted for as President, the House of Representatives shall choose immediately, by ballot, the President. But in choosing the President, the votes shall be taken by states, the representation from each state having one vote; a quorum for this purpose shall consist of a member or members from two-thirds of the states, and a majority of all the states shall be necessary to a choice. And if the House of Representatives shall not choose a President whenever the right of choice shall devolve upon them, before the fourth day of March next following, then the Vice-President shall act as President, as in the case of the death or other constitutional disability of the President. The person having the greatest number of votes as Vice-President, shall be the Vice-President, if such number be a majority of the whole number of electors appointed, and if no person have a majority, then from the two highest numbers on the list, the Senate shall choose the Vice-President; a quorum for the purpose shall consist of two-thirds of the whole number of Senators, and a majority of the whole number shall be necessary to a choice. But no person constitutionally ineligible to the office of President shall be eligible to that of Vice-President of the United States.

Amendment XIII

Passed by Congress January 31, 1865. Ratified December 6, 1865.

Section 1. Neither slavery nor involuntary servitude, except as a punishment for crime whereof the party shall have been duly convicted, shall exist within the United States, or any place subject to their jurisdiction.

Section 2. Congress shall have power to enforce this article by appropriate legislation.

Amendment XIV

Passed by Congress June 13, 1866. Ratified July 9, 1868.

Section 1. All persons born or naturalized in the United States, and subject to the jurisdiction thereof, are citizens of the United States and of the state wherein they reside. No state shall make or enforce any law which shall abridge the privileges or immunities of citizens of the United States; nor shall any state deprive any person of life, liberty, or property, without due process of law; nor deny to any person within its jurisdiction the equal protection of the laws.

Section 2. Representatives shall be apportioned among the several states according to their respective numbers, counting the whole number of persons in each state, excluding Indians not taxed. But when the right to vote at any election for the choice of electors for President and Vice President of the United States, Representatives in Congress, the executive and judicial officers of a state, or the members of the legislature thereof, is denied to any of the male inhabitants of such state, being twenty-one years of age, and citizens of the United States, or in any way abridged, except for participation in rebellion, or other crime, the basis of representation therein shall be reduced in the proportion which the number of such male citizens shall bear to the whole number of male citizens twenty-one years of age in such state.

Section 3. No person shall be a Senator or Representative in Congress, or elector of President and Vice President, or hold any office, civil or military, under the United States, or under any state, who, having previously taken an oath, as a member of Congress, or as an officer of the United States, or as a member of any state legislature, or as an executive or judicial officer of any state, to support the Constitution of the United States, shall have engaged in insurrection or rebellion against the same, or given aid or comfort to the enemies thereof. But Congress may by a vote of two-thirds of each House, remove such disability.

Section 4. The validity of the public debt of the United States, authorized by law, including debts incurred for payment of pensions and bounties for services in suppressing insurrection or rebellion, shall not be questioned. But neither the United States nor any state shall assume or pay any debt or obligation incurred in aid of insurrection or rebellion against the United States, or any claim for the loss or emancipation of any slave; but all such debts, obligations and claims shall be held illegal and void.

Section 5. The Congress shall have power to enforce, by appropriate legislation, the provisions of this article.

Amendment XV

Passed by Congress February 26, 1869. Ratified February 3, 1870.

Section 1. The right of citizens of the United States to vote shall not be denied or abridged by the United States or by any state on account of race, color, or previous condition of servitude.

Section 2. The Congress shall have power to enforce this article by appropriate legislation.

Amendment XVI

Passed by Congress July 2, 1909. Ratified February 3, 1913.

The Congress shall have power to lay and collect taxes on incomes, from whatever source derived, without apportionment among the several states, and without regard to any census or enumeration.

Amendment XVII

Passed by Congress May 13, 1912. Ratified April 8, 1913.

The Senate of the United States shall be composed of two Senators from each state, elected by the people thereof, for six years; and each Senator shall have one vote. The electors in each state shall have the qualifications requisite for electors of the most numerous branch of the state legislatures.

When vacancies happen in the representation of any state in the Senate, the executive authority of such state shall issue writs of election to fill such vacancies: Provided, that the legislature of any state may empower the executive thereof to make temporary appointments until the people fill the vacancies by election as the legislature may direct.

This amendment shall not be so construed as to affect the election or term of any Senator chosen before it becomes valid as part of the Constitution.

Amendment XVIII

Passed by Congress December 18, 1917. Ratified January 16, 1919.

Section 1. After one year from the ratification of this article the manufacture, sale, or transportation of intoxicating liquors within, the importation thereof into, or the exportation thereof from the United States and all territory subject to the jurisdiction thereof for beverage purposes is hereby prohibited.

Section 2. The Congress and the several states shall have concurrent power to enforce this article by appropriate legislation.

Section 3. This article shall be inoperative unless it shall have been ratified as an amendment to the Constitution by the legislatures of the several states, as provided in the Constitution, within seven years from the date of the submission hereof to the states by the Congress.

Amendment XIX

Passed by Congress June 4, 1919. Ratified August 18, 1920.

The right of citizens of the United States to vote shall not be denied or abridged by the United States or by any state on account of sex.

Congress shall have power to enforce this article by appropriate legislation.

Amendment XX

Passed by Congress March 2, 1932. Ratified January 23, 1933.

Section 1. The terms of the President and Vice President shall end at noon on the 20th day of January, and the terms of Senators and Representatives at noon on the 3d day of January, of the years in which such terms would have ended if this article had not been ratified; and the terms of their successors shall then begin.

Section 2. The Congress shall assemble at least once in every year, and such meeting shall begin at noon on the 3d day of January, unless they shall by law appoint a different day.

Section 3. If, at the time fixed for the beginning of the term of the President, the President elect shall have died, the Vice President elect shall become President. If a President shall not have been chosen before the time fixed for the beginning of his term, or if the President elect shall have failed to qualify, then the Vice President elect shall act as President until a President shall have qualified; and the Congress may by law provide for the case wherein neither a President elect nor a Vice President elect shall have qualified, declaring who shall then act as President, or the manner in which one who is to act shall be selected, and such person shall act accordingly until a President or Vice President shall have qualified.

Section 4. The Congress may by law provide for the case of the death of any of the persons from whom the House of Representatives may choose a President whenever the right of choice shall have devolved upon them, and for the case of the death of any of the persons from whom the Senate may choose a Vice President whenever the right of choice shall have devolved upon them.

Section 5. Sections 1 and 2 shall take effect on the 15th day of October following the ratification of this article.

Section 6. This article shall be inoperative unless it shall have been ratified as an amendment to the Constitution by the legislatures of three-fourths of the several states within seven years from the date of its submission.

Amendment XXI

Passed by Congress February 20, 1933. Ratified December 5, 1933.

Section 1. The eighteenth article of amendment to the Constitution of the United States is hereby repealed.

Section 2. The transportation or importation into any state, territory, or possession of the United States for delivery or use therein of intoxicating liquors, in violation of the laws thereof, is hereby prohibited.

Section 3. This article shall be inoperative unless it shall have been ratified as an amendment to the Constitution by conventions in the several states, as provided in the Constitution, within seven years from the date of the submission hereof to the states by the Congress.

Amendment XXII

Passed by Congress March 21, 1947. Ratified February 27, 1951.

Section 1. No person shall be elected to the office of the President more than twice, and no person who has held the office of President, or acted as President, for more than two years of a term to which some other person was elected President shall be elected to the office of the President more than once. But this article shall not apply to any person holding the office of President when this article was proposed by the Congress, and shall not prevent any person who may be holding the office of President, or acting as President, during the term within which this article becomes operative from holding the office of President or acting as President during the remainder of such term.

Section 2. This article shall be inoperative unless it shall have been ratified as an amendment to the Constitution by the legislatures of three-fourths of the several states within seven years from the date of its submission to the states by the Congress.

Amendment XXIII

Passed by Congress June 16, 1960. Ratified March 29, 1961.

Section 1. The District constituting the seat of government of the United States shall appoint in such manner as the Congress may direct:

A number of electors of President and Vice President equal to the whole number of Senators and Representatives in Congress to which the District would be entitled if it were a state, but in no event more than the least populous state; they shall be in addition to those appointed by the states, but they shall be considered, for the purposes of the election of President and Vice President, to be electors appointed by a state; and they shall meet in the District and perform such duties as provided by the twelfth article of amendment.

Section 2. The Congress shall have power to enforce this article by appropriate legislation.

Amendment XXIV

Passed by Congress August 27, 1962. Ratified January 23, 1964.

Section 1. The right of citizens of the United States to vote in any primary or other election for President or Vice President, for electors for President or Vice President, or for Senator or Representative in Congress, shall not be denied or abridged by the United States or any state by reason of failure to pay any poll tax or other tax.

Section 2. The Congress shall have power to enforce this article by appropriate legislation.

Amendment XXV

Passed by Congress July 6, 1965. Ratified February 10, 1967.

Section 1. In case of the removal of the President from office or of his death or resignation, the Vice President shall become President.

Section 2. Whenever there is a vacancy in the office of the Vice President, the President shall nominate a Vice President who shall take office upon confirmation by a majority vote of both Houses of Congress.

Section 3. Whenever the President transmits to the President pro tempore of the Senate and the Speaker of the House of Representatives his written declaration that he is unable to discharge the powers and duties of his office, and until he transmits to them a written declaration to the contrary, such powers and duties shall be discharged by the Vice President as Acting President.

Section 4. Whenever the Vice President and a majority of either the principal officers of the executive departments or of such other body as Congress may by law provide, transmit to the President pro tempore of the Senate and the Speaker of the House of Representatives their written declaration that the President is unable to discharge the powers and duties of his office, the Vice President shall immediately assume the powers and duties of the office as Acting President.

Thereafter, when the President transmits to the President pro tempore of the Senate and the Speaker of the House of Representatives his written declaration that no inability exists, he shall resume the powers and duties of his office unless the Vice President and a majority of either the principal officers of the executive department or of such other body as Congress may by law provide, transmit within four days to the President pro tempore of the Senate and the Speaker of the House of Representatives their written declaration that the President is unable to discharge the powers and duties of his office. Thereupon Congress shall decide the issue, assembling within forty-eight hours for that purpose if not in session. If the Congress, within twenty-one days after receipt of the latter written declaration, or, if Congress is not in session, within twenty-one days after Congress is required to assemble, determines by two-thirds vote of both Houses that the President is unable to discharge the powers and duties of his office, the Vice President shall continue to discharge the same as Acting President; otherwise, the President shall resume the powers and duties of his office.

Amendment XXVI

Passed by Congress March 23, 1971. Ratified June 30, 1971.

Section 1. The right of citizens of the United States, who are 18 years of age or older, to vote, shall not be denied or abridged by the United States or any state on account of age.

Section 2. The Congress shall have the power to enforce this article by appropriate legislation.

Amendment XXVII

Passed by Congress September 25, 1989. Ratified May 7, 1992.

No law, varying the compensation for the services of the Senators and Representatives, shall take effect, until an election of Representatives shall have intervened.